HOLLOW
POINT

HOLLOW
POINT

SEAN SWOGGER

atmosphere press

© 2022 Sean Swogger

Published by Atmosphere Press

Cover design by Matthew Fielder

No part of this book may be reproduced without permission from the author except in brief quotations and in reviews.

atmospherepress.com

TABLE OF CONTENTS

Zoom Sessions with God / 3

Hollow Point / 4

Occupy Heaven / 5

Passing George Floyd Mural on the Brown Line / 6

Shoot / 7

Chardon / 11

Shouldn't Try / 12

Nothin' like drinkin' / 13

Vegas / 14

Comeback Kids / 15

A Comprehensive List of Crisis Actors / 16

Sandy Hook / 17

623,471 / 21

After Roe / 22

Suicide Pact at my Alma Mater / 23

Ode to Li Wenliang / 24

Rehearsal / 25

Streetless People / 26

Science calls them / 27

Social Distancing / 28

Virginia Tech / 29

You Showed Me Once / 30

The Man, Man! / 31

A shining city on a hill / 32

Tonight I am Drunk / 33

Making the Most of a Global Quarantine / 34

American Carnage (Inaugural Edition 2017) / 35

Musty Couch (1975-2017) / 39

San Bernardino / 40

Winter of Peril / 41

Elegy for my First Wedding Ring / 42

And You Were Flawless / 43

Picture of Me Standing on the Shores of Lake Erie / 44

Eloping in January / 45

Stow, Ohio / 46

You Showed Me Twice / 47

We Stopped Praying in Schools! / 48

Aurora / 49

Only Temporary / 50

Pittsburgh / 51

Believing Cara / 52

Time's Up / 53

You (never) taught me / 54

The shining city on a hill / 55

Birth Control / 59

Another Way to Kill / 60

American Carnage (Live from The Capitol, 1/6/2021) / 61

Ted Cruz Speaks / 62

Parkland / 63

~~indictment of shooters dead/alive~~ / 64

Rigor Civilis / 65

My Little Microchip / 66

This shining city on a hill / 67

You Showed Me Over and Over and Over / 68

Centralia, Pennsylvania / 69

Crawl / 70

ZOOM SESSIONS WITH GOD

if only he was unmuted instead
of unfazed
if only he could reckon
not watch

I wish mom was right
on thunder nights
God is bowling
read: ignoring

wind is breath
an exodus from the lungs
but he answers:

*I will show wonders in the heavens
and in the earth: blood, fire,
and pillars of smoke.*

And I ask:
How do You live with Yourself?

Hollow Point

There's an echo
in the halls of Congress.
Podiums un-manned
or might as well be
until the departure of America's
very stable genius very
manly so manly
no mask is needed
lest we look like snowflakes
lest our lungs have snowflake shaped
x-rays endless x-rays boundless damage from co-
dependent Congress liars
the authors of this great American carnage
kids raptured by bullets
over and over raptured
by inaction
by talking points
hollow points hollow points hollow

Occupy Heaven

5.56?
Round up to six feet, God.

Check your Pulse,
we're gonna dance the night away.
Free round after free round for you, babe.

More victims are here, Jesus observes
from a window as Peter's gate crashes open.
Should we tell them? The Prophet shakes his head
as they turn to the throne, removing the gun from God's hand.

Great show man, delay
the finale for machine gun applause.

Blood and Soil,
Coming to a synagogue near you.

Behind God's throne, gray matter hangs on the wall
like a first grader's backpack on the hooks by her cubby

Jesus leaps back as a rock smashes the window.
Confucius picks it from the floor,
inspecting its granite grooves.

Buddha turns his eye from the peephole,
deadlocking the palace door. *They'll want answers.*

All eyes fall to God's corpse,
his white robes, white beard stained
red with bloody broken teeth.
Slumping over his father, Jesus weeps.

Lucifer rises from a murky, coagulating pool.
Wine from tears, anybody?

Boots crunch on glass outside
like bones under a Manhattan pickup truck.

You're as guilty as the rest of us, Christ cries.

I only tempt, friend. Lucifer points at the mangled body.
He created.

Passing George Floyd Mural on the Brown Line

There are still holes
in the walls of Gettysburg
drums are beating
in the walls of Gettysburg
my foot taps the train
taps the coffin of Lincoln
taps tomorrow
taps time
I miss my stop
you smile from a crumbling wall
ash and copper surround
your crumbling face
I say your name
I am a chorus
your painted smile
doesn't change
my foot taps the train
taps the coffin of an elephant
traps tomorrow
traps time.

Shoot

the shit
for the moon
a look
a gaze
a glare
a load
daggers
heroin
BBs
an arrow
a target
a deer
a man
a woman
my father, a teacher
my kindergarten sister
you
a child.

Chardon

I didn't understand what a school shooting was
until we heard about Chardon.
Shocking, sure, but it could never happen
here.
Chardon is close, but still isn't
home.

In the study hall at 7:30 am among friends
this kid, only seventeen
walks right in with a handgun.
A small thing—only a .22

Wikipedia (I know, right) tells me they're
the most common round in the world
low cost
minimal recoil
minimal noise

"ideal cartridge"
for recreational shooting
initial firearms training
small-game hunting
pest control.

That's what we are to all you leaders, right?
Pretty hard for new generations to learn
or fight for change if they're dead
Gotta preserve your power somehow.

Shouldn't Try

They call
me the Seatbelt
Snipper
and I'm gonna
make road safety great again.
If you're gonna die
with a seatbelt,
you don't need one—
it ain't like they'll
save every single life.

I ignore the "employees must wash hands" signs
tryna make immune systems great again.
Might as well prevent that autism, too—
those vaccines can't stop every virus,
so many of them in disgusting hospitals.

Nothin' like drinkin'

on a brown line train
slumped against the glass.
The skyline is visible from the platform
I pretend to need a breath of fresh air
so the mask comes off
I make sure to throw my voice
so hard it shakes the city
and I know you hear me
but you turn away instead
mask on your ears.

My brown line train passes by your window
you're on the red line looking for hope
that we can make a difference
I think we'll end at the same stop
despite setbacks and the fog
of propaganda
we can reach the same spot
in different ways
without reading each other's
maps, reading lines, reading
thighs. Can anyone breathe
in surgical masks?
I believe we will.

Vegas

No bump stocks?
He would just use regular rifles!

No rifles?
Handguns!

Spears, knives, javelins, shotput, Molotov cocktails, beer bottles, broken glass, broken glass beer bottles, branches, toothpicks, sharpened graphite pencils, custom-made chairs, cars, IEDs, inaction, obesity, heart conditions, lack of healthcare, trash bags, weaponized shark teeth, excessive carpet burn, lighter-air freshener combo, MacGyver-meets-Rambo type shit.

Thank you for your hypothesis, please
select an option from the word bank above.

Using evidence, please
explain how your choice
would kill
more than 59 people
and injure 422 people.

In 9-11 minutes

From the 32nd floor

Please.

Comeback Kids

This morning
I am high
binge-watching John Mulaney stand-up specials
instead of trying
to write about mass shootings
because I'm too afraid to face the bodies—
photos
of Sandy Hook children
in first grade.

Tomorrow
I will tell myself
that I have no choice
if I want to respect them
because it could have been any
of my three sisters.

A Comprehensive List of Crisis Actors

Alex Jones: You are the most mentally ill people I've ever seen, wanting to gang-rape this Republic and this country and the West. *Stephen Miller:* I will do things that no one else in their right mind would do. *Steve Bannon:* I'd actually like to go back to Tudor England, I'd put the heads on pikes, right, I'd put them at the two corners of the White House as a warning. *Matt Gaetz:* How many women rallying for Roe are over-educated, under-loved millennials who sadly return from protests to a lonely microwave dinner with their cats, and no bumble matches? *Roger Stone:* Prepare to die cocksucker. *Kevin McCarthy:* I don't think anybody is challenging the legitimacy of the presidential election. *Mitch McConnell:* You must be under the mistaken impression that I care.

Sandy Hook

Will you pick the shells off the floor
like flowers in the woods?

Take my picture by the red maple tree.

Click.

Make a leaf print scrapbook
so you can trace your fingers
along the vein of each flower.

Pretend the baby veins are mine
once my handprint fades
in the sand, on the wall
from when I dipped my hand
into a bucket of red paint
and smeared it, and smeared the light switch

Click.

so you could remember me
every time you tucked me in
and turned out the light, goodnight.

623,471

Legal abortions in 2016.
Libruls ain't stopping those deaths.
Don't even care about
their own snowflake-sized embryos.

Ya know
there needs to be some kind of education center.
A place to plan for parenthood or
at least tell 'em how to prevent pregnancy.

Maybe they could do other shit—
breast cancer screening,
Pap tests,
pregnancy tests,
prenatal services,
treatment for sexually transmitted infection?

Let's call it Snowflake Prevention.

After Roe

Like a monster
hungry
under the bed
hungry
rights for sale
hungry

The monster called America feeds because it cannot fill itself with dreams
or no longer wants to.

The monster called America chews its food because it cannot swallow us all at once
incremental gnashing is best for the gut.

And it does take guts
forcing my sisters back into the alley so the miscarriage does not kill them too.

It does take guts to turn away from stairs
the ones your sister throws herself down with a child of rape
because her body is her own.

The women we love are nobody in the monster's eyes.
The girls they're forced to have will become women that are nobody in the monster's black eyes.

I think my mother is somebody.
I think my sisters are somebody.
I think my wife is somebody.

Are you somebody?

The monster called America is already considering its next meal
and it's probably you.

Suicide Pact at My Alma Mater

I didn't know you,
I was a sophomore at the same school
class of '13.

My locker combination was 6-15-45.
Kids used to jam their lockers with pen caps.
As a freshman, I'd walk around and pull them out.
I treated some people like shit at the lunch table.

Would that have pushed you over the edge?

Maybe it's better that I wasn't there
as much as I think I could have helped.

I played Willy Wonka.
I used Puffenberger Hall's projector
to ask a girl to Senior Prom.
I know your life wasn't easy,
that nobody can relate.
I know it's never easy.
I take three pills a day for Bipolar II.
I write.

ODE TO LI WENLIANG

Wuhan doctor dead at 33
dismissed as a rumor monger
threatened by the state
forced to sign a statement that his warning was illegal behavior.

Li started showing symptoms
so like any liar would, he booked a hotel room
to avoid infecting his pregnant wife and son
with a "false" disease.

They could have listened
could have strangled COVID in its crib
he could have lived to see his baby in its crib

Good news!
China declared him a martyr after his death
a hero, a great man, a whatever-makes-them-feel-better
a reason that 6,300,000 people didn't have to die
if they just fucking listened.

Rehearsal

The city cracks open as we cross the river. Shrinks to alleys between skyscrapers. There are protesters passing McDonald's beneath my train. They head toward the tower with a president's name, toward the line of riot shields and a bed you won't be murdered in.

Sitting on the train, peering through steamy glasses, resisting the urge to pull down my mask and wipe the humidity from my face. When the train passes behind a skyscraper, I lose sight of the protesters, the riot gear, the daily McDonald's deals, burning cars, "end is nigh" graffiti.

Rehearsing what I'll say if someone tries to sit next to me. For a moment, I lose sight of the difference between plague and person, between system and support. These rehearsals have a habit of being meaner and more aggressive than what I imagine, realistically, will come out. I will yell about keeping six feet away. Or my eyes will narrow, I will scowl and do nothing but sit on the sidelines.

STREETLESS PEOPLE

Narrow alleys
empty streets
farmers' markets
won't return
without masks

Abandoned stalls
where homemade pies
rot

Abandoned people
where phones
aren't answered
Missing poster
missing cat
missing people
missing search

SCIENCE CALLS THEM

organisms at the edge of life
no, not politicians—viruses
but like politicians they campaign
convincing your body
it doesn't have a choice
or a place in this new world
unless you help them stay in power
unless you help destroy institutions
that have kept you safe
for your entire life.

It's true that most people will be fine,
their cells will vote the virus out
perhaps by 7,000,000 votes
but sometimes the virus hangs on
refuses to leave, turns the institutions
against you.

These are the times when the virus must be excised—
cut out dragged out screaming defeated at all costs
because a single surviving virus will replicate
its influence will remain, perhaps overturning
important decisions you've made
a single surviving virus will mutate
and return to power far more dangerous than before.

Social Distancing

Dad texts me about every new case
instead of asking how my day went.

A student insists
these are the end times
I stay calm
explain this is the greatest time to be alive
by almost any metric.

I tell my students not to panic as tiny creatures at the edge of life
creep toward us, crippling countries and shuttering markets.

I say we're all going to be okay
as our campus considers
asking kids to stay home
and come to school via the internet.

I jokingly text my sister
asking if she's infected:
No
she says
but we did have an active shooter
drill.

I tell her not to panic,
but tomorrow
I'll shut
my key-coded classroom
just in case.

VIRGINIA TECH

If only the professors had weapons—

Actually, let's tackle that one right now.

Average price of a 9mm handgun: $325
9mm (1000 rounds): $150
20% of teachers qualified for firearms: 700,000

700,000(325+150) = $332,500,000

$475 per classroom for supplies and literally anything else that could help kids.

What a time to be alive
or not alive—dead students mean more money for survivors.
New backpacks?
Books?
Crayons?
Sisters?

You Showed Me Once

In the movies
you showed me
that using the Force to choke
holds them on the ground
helpless.

In a musical
you showed me
aiming at the sky
doesn't save you.

In the street
you showed me
toy guns turn real
when you're
Black and a child.

The Man, Man!

> With the right to bear arms comes a great responsibility to use caution and common sense on handgun purchases.
> —Ronald Reagan, 1991 Speech at George Washington University.

A well-regulated Militia…
Well, honey, it's time for me to hit the road for our militia meeting in case the government goes
bad. We have a militia for that, right?
It's regulated, isn't it?

…being necessary to the security of a free state…
In case we have to mount a resistance, mentally unstable people don't have access to weapons that might jeopardize our operations, right?

…the right of the people to keep and bear Arms…
You're saying that it's the right of the people to have a well-regulated militia? Honey, are our
rights being violated if we **don't** regulate this thing?

…shall not be infringed.
What do you mean, the 2nd Amendment was a change to the Constitution? You mean to tell me
that the Constitution of the United States can be changed? What if they take away our free
speech, too? No, honey, of course words aren't killing people at 45 rounds a minute.

But what if they try to steal free speech, anyway?
We should organize a well-regulated militia…

A SHINING CITY ON A HILL

only glows when the camera
shows me burning cars
your effigy your
enemy your
social distant
tear gas photo op
your motorcade you're
positive your
socialized medicine
Capitol hospital
thirteen doctor
doctored numbers
anti-deep you're
anti-state you're
anti-me you're
anti-cure you're
anti-blue you're
anti-science
anti-camera
anti-you

Tonight I am Drunk

head laid against the wall of this bathroom
proofreading a poster above the urinal
I can't correct anyway
stumbling for miles
between bed and refrigerator
table and laptop
tongue and trigger.

Making the Most of a Global Quarantine

Sleep in.
Wake up.
Go back to sleep.
Learn to make coffee via French Press.
Conduct all business from bed (PJs optional).
Watch a seventeen-year-old make
a website that tracks corona cases
as you fail to write anything for weeks.
Catch up on shows (clothing optional).
Let beard grow,
call it "quarantine beard"
despite having more time than ever to properly trim.
Listen to every Green Day album in chronologic,
alphabetic, backward order.
Write down favorite lyrics.
More coffee.
Weigh pros and cons of walking to grocery store.
Weigh self.
Proceed to grocery store.
Select favorite wine/beer.
Accidentally forget important item.
Forget to take bipolar meds;
days bleed together.
Exhaust music,
shows, games,
sleep

American Carnage (Inaugural Edition 2017)

When you open your heart
to patriotism, there is no room
for prejudice. The kids, they say,
"Wow, I will have my own bed.
I will sleep on the bed and I
will have a cabinet for my
clothes." Why are we having all
these people from shithole
countries coming here? Drug
dealers, criminals, rapists. These
aren't people, they're animals.
So go home. We love you.
You're very special.

Musty Couch (1975-2017)

I was hungry, living in the basement
of a lawyer's office.
Back when there was no food,
when money meant fingering
the sofa, meant unzipping
stained, vomit-green cushions
as if crumbs from the early Eighties
would sustain me, sustain me
like my Looney Toons blankie
from the late Nineties, which I'd lose in St. Louis
during the family's 2002 summer vacation.
I should've known that things would go
south when a Midwest monsoon held us up
near the Mississippi,
flooding everything in sight
with its murky, half-digested innards.

My apartment flooded, once.
Water needs food too, and so
it fingered my lungs,
fell asleep inside me.
Turned me green,
turned the couch black,
but before the mold set in,
the couch exuded a single polaroid picture.
In fading colors, both my uncle and I had fallen
asleep on the couch. No more than two years old,
I was wrapped in my Looney Toons blankie.

I slept on those cushions for decades,
slept inside my blankie, my uncle's embrace,
inside empty bottles either spilled
or sucked dry (milk and otherwise).
I soaked her with beer and bile and come
and go and stay and sleep.

Tonight
After I've called my uncle a traitor
for supporting a coup
I sleep on soggy carpet.
Sustain me.

SAN BERNARDINO

Build that wall
of thoughts
so we can stop
white bullets
better yet, let's deport 800,000 Dreamers
with a million prayers
God only knows when they'll start shooting us
wait
no
let's ban all the Muslims
that'll stop
insatiable whites
from
slaughtering
children
no
no I've got it
what if we march them
into internment camps
like the Japanese?
March
them
into uncharted territory.
#ThoughtsandPrayers

Winter of Peril

It wasn't *my* anniversary party.

We watched Aunt Marion visit every table. We watched every maskless Ohioan
greet her, kiss her. We whispered in the car about this being the last time we'll ever
see her.

Dad told us Mr. Rair was hospitalized after subbing for a high school class, about how he was hospitalized so long he had to relearn how to walk.

Floyd was on a ventilator but you can't see your friends.
Kylie's first patient still can't breathe.

One of my students went back to work for the first time in three months. Tom thinks he'll lose
his job this week. Your glasses fog up when you wear a mask.

Elegy for My First Wedding Ring

All I wanted
was to resize you
remember to shop local
during the pandemic
they said
well
why not the local jeweler
why not answer their phone call
the ring must be ready
how about you come in and take a look
they said
shit
put on mask
coat
gloves
put on boots
put on poker face
ring doorbell
enter store's airlock
stare at statue of Mary
beside busty Eighties model mags
Mayan murals, disembodied
voice behind shelf
shelf behind counter
how're you doing
he said
and that was the last conversation I had
before he handed me
a ruined ring.

And You Were Flawless

Today I am vulnerable. The Citalopram, Buproprion, Lamotrigine may not be working, though "working" is a relative term. If my cycles have gone from 1.5 months to a few days of existing at the bottom or flying high, I suppose the meds work.

Today I am on edge like I might lash out at those fuckers in the corner opening their mouths to
step on the teacher's toes.

I dreamt of you in your fuzzy purple socks and black silk underwear. I bet it's because I've been listening to My Chemical Romance—your favorite band. I even started listening to your favorite album—the one I couldn't stand aside from "I'm Not Okay."

You picked Saint Helena to be your confirmation name. As far as my research goes, she was the mother of Constantine. What can I say, I fall in love with strong women and liars.

Picture of Me Standing on the Shores of Lake Erie

I miss you during cold nights
when my breath forms clouds
and I struggle to peer through
self-made steam.

Between moon
and horizon.
I hang from stars,
climbing toward dawn.
Slip into icy midnight.
My lungs forge clouds
and break my fall.

I stand on the shores
of Lake Erie,
belts of ice and slush.
How far could I go
before I am inhaled
by fissures?

Eloping in January

My Capitol was attacked.
Kylie's car buried in foot of snow.
President impeached (again).
Witnessed five-car crash.

Kylie's car buried in foot of snow.
Applied for teaching jobs.
Witnessed five-car crash.
90,000 dead from virus.

Applied for teaching jobs.
I proposed.
90,000 dead from virus.
She said yes.

I proposed.
Capitol attacked.
She said yes.
Capitol attacked.

Stow, Ohio

There are towns I only know because Dick
Goddard at Fox 8 News warned of tornadoes nearby,
of hook echoes and hail, microbursting squall lines.
I sat and saw the eighty-eight counties of Ohio
turn yellow, turn red, watched until grandma stuffed me in a
closet when dad left to chase
after funnel clouds again.

Goddard, 88 now, looks a bit like grandpa
if he had lived to the same age.

Grandpa, 78 then, dropped dead in the shower
from a flash flood heart attack—the smell
of another burnt batch of cookies in the updraft
from grandma's oven—so sudden I had to wonder
if the charred, smoldering scent
rekindled an Auschwitz odor
out of his nightmares to ask
why he didn't just get there sooner.

Ten years later, Goddard worked in the Pacific,
forecasting atmospheric effects of nuclear tests
Grandpa "made parts fer nukes"
during the second Red Scare,
watching yellow countries turn red,
watching grandma dance
the nuclear shuffle
dance my dad into the closet
when the sirens howled.

I'm in their closet listening to sirens howl,
to the wind whip the branches,
to Dick Goddard whisper
from the living room to seek shelter.
Grandma's cookies are burning.

You Showed Me Twice

In Akron
you showed me
a Black man
can be the greatest
of
all time
if he plays ball
and stays in his lane.

In Kent
you showed me
national guards
aren't
always
national.

In California
you showed me
fires that swallow
any
doubt.

WE STOPPED PRAYING IN SCHOOLS!

God is punishing us!
We've been asking for it since 1962
when the damned libs ruled against us in the Supreme Court.

Before that
praying in school saved
six million from concentration camps
and another *sixty* million in the war!

It's the reason that Spanish Flu didn't kill
75,000,000 people back in 1918.

And during the Civil War,
it saved 685,000 Americans from slaughtering each other.

But ever since we stopped praying
220,000 have died
from an orange
god's panic.

Aurora

Would you be Batman
or the Joker?

The scene where he dresses up
like a nurse?

Does Batman ever ignore the bat signal?

What if Wayne Enterprises actually profits
from the criminals?

If Bruce asked us to buy 700,000 rifles
that Wayne Enterprises produced,
would anyone bat an eye?

Only Temporary

I've ordered a box
that now sits
soggy in the rain
in the front
by the mailbox.

The box is full
of food I've ordered
from digital chains
of digital food
in electric circles
of life.

With no internet I looked inside
my Wi-Fi box
expecting a dark room
where magic happens
where God might
be.

PITTSBURGH

Shabbat Shalom means you're wishing somebody peace on
Saturday. Not mailing bombs to Democrats—the post office closes
at noon, anyway. Not buying ammunition. Not making sure
your weapons are in perfect working order.

Peace on Saturday—sent into the eternal peace, he must have
thought.
Maybe they even said it before he started mowing them down.
Peace on Saturday, "the most horrific crime scene I've ever seen,"
says the city chief.

Can this be finished if there's a new shooting every other day?
Is my voice worth any of the air it'll use to shout for attention?

Believing Cara

Why didn't I see the predator
when I was his teaching assistant
when I always
thought
he was full of shit
over the top

when he offered girls
agents
offered to string
along students
peers
wife
kids

dear rapist
dear worthless
dear fake tears
ray bradbury isn't proud of you
isn't proud of you
isn't proud of you
worthless

Time's Up

He touched her
touched me
broke you
broke down
broken
back down
retreat
refuse
defense
distraught
same room
his face
me
her
break him
break me
break
them

You (Never) Taught Me

In the classroom
you (never) taught me
the FBI tried to make
Martin Luther King Jr.
commit
suicide.

You (never) taught me
we sleep in monochrome
Americans dream in White
Americans nightmare in Black.

You (never) taught me
about fire swallowing
the richest
Black
community
in the country.

THE SHINING CITY ON A HILL

is a burial mound
in Ohio. A serpent
mound of bodies tread on by white
destiny
a meteor crater
medicine manifested
in a white streak of sky
a serpent in the sky
shining in the sky
tread on by white
beard
white
robes
white
gods
white
time.

Birth Control

I scream at Christ:
my voice travels up, up, up
and bounces off his front door.
What an asshole.

Deceitful Daisy,
Runaway saint who sold me up, up, up
the river, smothering infidelity
with your body.

"Fuck off," she said, putting my
withered chassis in neutral,
lurching-forward leaning-back,
yelping that we aren't going up, up,
in flames as we choke
back tears: Blame the smoke
not the spark, she begs, begs, begs
between moans.
Water balloons won't put you out, honey.
You're a fucking wildfire.

I *let* you slam my door last night
so the bottle I threw wouldn't shatter on your back.
I didn't *mean* to get your hopes up to think I might chase,
but I won't enable *another* fit of madness.

I made my stand that night—
you made your own and climbed
from the hood of your Elantra and
up, up, up the ledge
of Parking Deck North.

Just as my temples touched the pillow,
your lips caressed concrete.
I prayed you wouldn't get pregnant.
You leapt up, up, up to God's front door
and knocked.

Another Way to Kill

A shooter
an archer
and a swordsman walk into a bar.

The swordsman
decked out in a Samurai's kimono
deflects an arrow like a Jedi
strikes the archer
disemboweling him.

The shooter
with his Kevlar vest
500 rounds
and a bump stock
shoots the swordsman,
then kills everyone in the bar.

AMERICAN CARNAGE (LIVE AT THE CAPITOL, 1/6/2021)

I only need 11,000 votes. Fellas, I
need 11,000 votes. Gimme a break.
Let's have trial by combat.
Because you'll never take back our
country with weakness. We fight
like Hell and if you don't fight
like Hell, you're not going to have
a country anymore. You have to
show strength and you have to
be strong. I hope you're going to
stand up for the good of our
Constitution and for the good of
our country. And if you're not, I'm
going to be very disappointed in
you.

TED CRUZ SPEAKS

Donald Trump: Grab 'em by the pussy. You can do anything. *Ted Cruz*: You mess with my wife, you mess with my kids; that'll do it every time. Donald, you're a sniveling coward and leave Heidi the hell alone. *Donald Trump*: Would you be willing to argue the case [about overturning the 2020 election]. *Ted Cruz*: Sure, I'd be happy to.

Parkland

There's no message hidden here.

Fix the fucking problem
or Gen Z—the brats
who think they're entitled to life,
who disrespect failed laws,
will do it for you.
Isn't that what you raised us to do?
"If there's a problem, ya fix it."
Then again, you could keep standing there
waving your dick for money
since it's easier than taking action.

You're telling me that children should be slaughtered so you can have more money?
The 2nd Amendment is an *amendment*—a change to the Constitution,
because you're allowed to change it.

When's the last time you saw an actual militia of civilians protecting America with hunting
rifles, handguns, and AR-15s? There's a white militia. A white one that does nothing when a
Black man is murdered for legally owning a weapon.

Have a great time shooting at an Abrams tank or an F16 fighter
when the government goes evil

.

~~INDICTMENT OF SHOOTERS DEAD/ALIVE~~

~~some survivors have chosen to forgive you, to feel sorry for you.~~
~~they're bigger people than I am.~~

~~I burned every fucking picture of you~~
~~so I could taste the way you'll burn in the deepest parts of hell~~
~~and for those who don't believe in hell, nothing but the eternal~~
~~void~~
~~of unconsciousness~~
~~you earned it.~~

~~your names aren't important. your lives weren't important.~~
~~you'll be remembered as a nameless group of perpetrators~~
~~who made this country a safer place when we finally said~~
~~"enough."~~

you
don't
deserve
attention

Rigor Civilis

A dry-erase calendar on the refrigerator
a bubble marks the month of February
The 9th-15th are listed.
The twelfth is marked "Sean's bday"
but my birthday is in March.

Here, even time is on a ventilator

Dinner plans are listed:
soup, burgers, polenta,
tacos
chicken, pork.

An unmailed package
sleeps on the floor
thousand-piece puzzles
destined for my mother
intended for shipping weeks ago.

A laundry basket
clean clothes near the bed,
still waiting
to hang.

The fire alarm beeps
every
thirty
seconds.

No butter by the microwave
but smears on the glass tray,
white specks multiplying throughout.

New sticks in the fridge
right next to the mildew.

Open door.
Retrieve wet paper towel.
Begin
to wipe
clean.

My Little Microchip

Baby, you'd put billionaires
out of business
if the world knew your richness.

They call you the mark of the beast
but you can be my priest.
Get out of my phone

and into me.
Don't ever let me be.
Here's where I go every day,

you'll never be far away.
Let's run away together—
they'll never know the love we treasure

THIS SHINING CITY ON A HILL

told me
a couple kids have to die
to protect our ~~best~~
second best
right,
right?

You Showed Me Over and Over and Over

In America
you showed me
bad cops aren't bad
for good cops.

In America
you showed me
guns are illegal
when guns are Black.

In America
you showed me fire
is the only language
we speak.

Centralia, Pennsylvania

Centralia's population has dwindled from more than 1,000 residents in 1980 to 63 by 1990, to only five in 2017—a result of the coal mine fire which has been burning beneath the borough since 1962.

A boy fell today
the ground shifted
a sinkhole dilated
in the backyard.
Good thing his cousin
was here to play today.
Good thing the tire-swing tree
wasn't swallowed today.
As the boy clung to its roots
150 feet above death
did he wonder why
his town let the coal seams burn
for longer than he'd been alive.

CRAWL

out of your window on the second floor
and sit on the roof with me
bring that shitty vodka
in the plastic jug
watch the crowds
stand in the wind tunnel
of our street
water rain
bean bag hail
tear gas fog
umbrellas for faces
crawl out of their mouths
and sit on the concrete coasts
because you can't breathe
with lungs that no longer scream
for more.

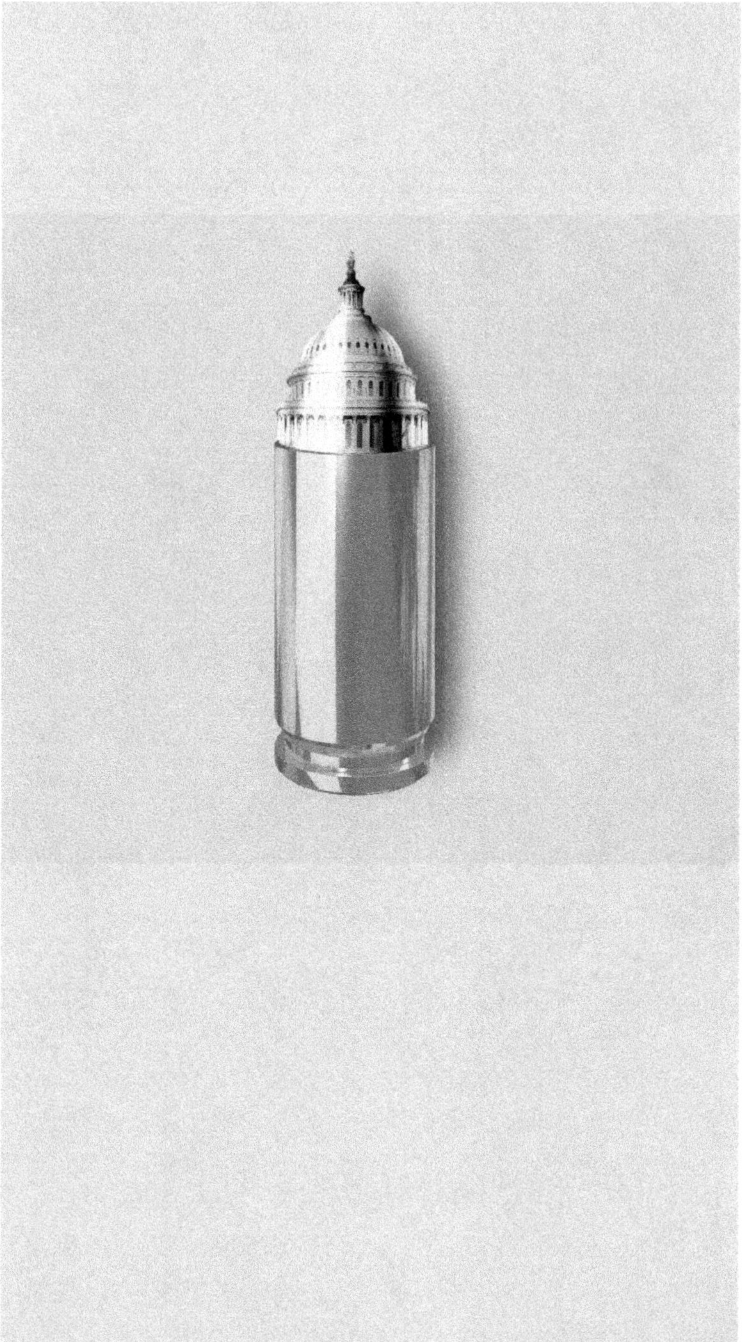

Acknowledgments

Endless thanks to the anthologies and journals kind enough to publish some of these poems in one form or another:

"Birth Control," *Sink Hollow*; "Occupy Heaven" (as "Ode to America"), *The Poet's Haven Digest: Darker Than Fiction Anthology*; "Shoot," *MASKS Literary Magazine*; "A Shining City on a Hill," "The Shining City on a Hill," and "Stow, Ohio," *Allium, A Journal of Poetry and Prose*.

Gratitude also to the generous friends willing to read this over and over and over again. I wouldn't be writing poems without Bob King. I wouldn't be writing poems at this level without my cohort —Castor, Ito, Lauren, Nisha, and Tracie—or without the gifted professors at Columbia College Chicago, especially Tony Trigilio, David Trinidad, and CM Burroughs.

Notes

"Chardon"
Chardon, Ohio, 02/27/2012. Three killed, three wounded in roughly a minute by shooter with .22 handgun.

"Vegas"
Las Vegas, Nevada, 10/01/2017. Sixty killed, eight-hundred sixty-seven wounded in ten minutes by shooter with twenty-three rifles, one revolver.

"A Comprehensive List of Crisis Actors"
Poem remixes found material from a clip of Alex Jones discussing media friendliness to Islam; a comment made by Stephen Miller during a high school speech; comments from Steve Bannon's podcast; a text from Roger Stone; an interview with Kevin McCarthy; and Mitch McConnell's response to the merits of an Obama-backed bill.

"Sandy Hook"
Newton, Connecticut, 12/14/2012. Twenty-seven killed, two wounded in five minutes by shooter with one Bushmaster XM15-E2S rifle, one Glock 20SF handgun.

"Virginia Tech"
Blacksburg, Virginia, 04/16/2007. Thirty-two killed, twenty-three wounded by shooter with one Glock 19 handgun, one Walther P22 handgun during one attack at 7:30am (roughly one minute) and another at 9:40am (roughly ten minutes).

"American Carnage (Inaugural Edition, 2017)"
Poem remixes found material from Donald Trump's 2017 inaugural address (often referred to by journalists as Trump's "American Carnage speech"), along with found material from tape recordings of Melania Trump made by Stephanie Winston Wolkoff, the First Lady's former advisor; a 2018 Oval Office talk with senators about protecting immigrants; the 2015 speech which launched his campaign; a May 2018 conversation with Californian leaders on immigration; and from his videotaped remarks after his followers had stormed the United States Capitol.

"San Bernardino"
San Bernardino, California, 12/02/2015. Fourteen killed, twenty-four wounded in three minutes by shooter with two AR-15 style rifles, two semi-automatic handguns.

"Aurora"
Aurora, Colorado, 07/20/2012. Twelve killed, seventy wounded in seven minutes by shooter with one Smith & Wesson M&P15, one Remington 870 Express Tactical 12-gauge shotgun, one Glock 22 Gen4 handgun.

"Pittsburgh"
Pittsburgh, Pennsylvania, 10/27/2018. Eleven killed, six wounded in twenty minutes by shooter with AR-15 style rifle, three Glock .357 SIG handguns.

"American Carnage (Live at the Capitol, 1/6/2021)"
Poem remixes found material from President Trump's rally inciting his followers to march on the Capitol, and Georgia Secretary of State Brad Raffensperger's January 2, 2021, phone call with President Trump.

"Ted Cruz Speaks"
Poem remixes found material from a taped conversation of Donald Trump; Ted Cruz's response to Trump after Trump attacked Cruz's wife for her looks; and a conversation between Cruz and Trump about plans to argue at the Supreme Court to overturn the results of the legitimate 2020 presidential election, against which Trump had already filed and lost at least 63 lawsuits.

"Parkland"
Parkland, Florida, 02/14/2018. Seventeen killed, seventeen wounded in six minutes by shooter with Smith & Wesson M&P15.

"Suicide Pact at my Alma Mater"
Jackson, Ohio, 02/23/2018. Murder-suicide of two high school students.

About Atmosphere Press

Atmosphere Press is an independent, full-service publisher for excellent books in all genres and for all audiences. Learn more about what we do at atmospherepress.com.

We encourage you to check out some of Atmosphere's latest releases, which are available at Amazon.com and via order from your local bookstore:

Until the Kingdom Comes, poetry by Jeanne Lutz

Warcrimes, poetry by GOODW.Y.N

The Freedom of Lavenders, poetry by August Reynolds

Convalesce, poetry by Enne Zale

Poems for the Bee Charmer (And Other Familiar Ghosts), poetry by Jordan Lentz

Serial Love: When Happily Ever After... Isn't, poetry by Kathy Kay

Flowers That Die, poetry by Gideon Halpin

Through The Soul Into Life, poetry by Shoushan

Embrace The Passion In A Lover's Dream, poetry by Paul Turay

Reflections in the Time of Trumpius Maximus, poetry by Mark Fishbein

Drifters, poetry by Stuart Silverman

As a Patient Thinks about the Desert, poetry by Rick Anthony Furtak

Winter Solstice, poetry by Diana Howard

Blindfolds, Bruises, and Break-Ups, poetry by Jen Schneider

Songs of Snow and Silence, poetry by Jen Emery

INHABITANT, poetry by Charles Crittenden

Godless Grace, poetry by Michael Terence O'Brien

March of the Mindless, poetry by Thomas Walrod

About the Author

Sean Swogger (he/him) grew up in Canal Fulton, Ohio and graduated from Kent State University at Stark in 2017 before receiving his MFA in Poetry from Columbia College Chicago in 2021. He currently works with disability services in higher education. In his spare time, Sean enjoys failing to train his new kittens.

CPSIA information can be obtained
at www.ICGtesting.com
Printed in the USA
LVHW101339300523
748296LV00006B/927

9 781639 888276